Instructional Literature for Middle-Level Band

Compiled and edited by Edward J. Kvet

MENC **Music Educators National Conference**

Contents

Introduction

A common dilemma faced by band educators is finding quality literature for young bands. Most educators can recite a so-called "standard repertoire" for band. However, this list rarely contains Grade 1–3 selections that are appropriate for middle-level bands. As a means of filling this void, this project was undertaken at the urging of Charles Hoffer, MENC past president, during his term as chair of the MENC Publications Planning Committee.

The task was straightforward: develop not only a list of quality literature for middle-level bands, but find out *why* experienced middle-level band educators believe these are quality selections and *what* specific skills they teach with each selection. All too often, educators perform certain literature simply because it "sounds good" or is new, rather than making the selection on the basis of what instructional skills or concepts can be taught.

It is with this purpose in mind that selected middle-level band educators were asked to submit their "top ten" selections appropriate for middle-level bands (Grade 1–3). These submissions were edited to maintain a similar format while keeping the comments of the reviewer in their own words. The following middle-level band educators are thanked for their participation in this project: Tonya Broyles-Brouillard, Oconomowoc, Wisconsin; Dixie Detgen, Buchanan, Michigan; Kenneth Feneley, Clare, Michigan; Ted Hadley, Twin Falls, Idaho; David Reul, Oconomowoc, Wisconsin; Nancy Sieloff-Ruebke, Flint, Michigan; William Sutherland, Charlotte, Michigan; and Marguerite Wilder, Smyrna, Georgia.

This publication is intended to be used as a resource by middle-level band educators and students in college-level methods and materials courses. It should be an especially valuable resource for first- and second-year educators who are looking for quality literature to help their middle-level students learn specific skills and concepts and meet the standards set forth in the *National Standards for Arts*

Education (MENC, 1994). It could also provide follow-up materials for some of the strategies provided in the forthcoming publication *Strategies for Teaching Beginning and Intermediate Band.*

Educators are urged to use this publication in conjunction with *Teaching Wind and Percussion Instruments: A Course of Study* (MENC, 1991) and *The School Music Program: A New Vision* (MENC, 1994) to assist in developing sequenced learning outcomes to meet their local needs. Rather than a complete listing of middle-level band literature, this document attempts to provide a representative list or "starting point" for middle-level band educators. No endorsement of any particular composer or publisher is intended or should be inferred.

Level 1–1½

Title: Anasazi
Level/Grade: 1
Composer/Arranger: John Edmondson
Publisher: Queenwood
Classification: Overture
Duration: 2:30

Instrumentation: Standard

Specific Requirements/Considerations: No problems

Instructional Concepts/Skills: Crescendo/decrescendo; breath control and line

General Comments: Effective at evoking a mood, this piece is a wonderful Grade 1 selection that students enjoy.

—Submitted by Ted Hadley

Title: Bist Du Bei Mir
Level/Grade: 1
Composer/Arranger: Bach/McGinty
Publisher: Queenwood
Classification: Chorale
Duration: 2:00

Instrumentation: Clarinet and trumpet are divided 2 ways. Low brass and woodwinds are unison. Trumpet range is to D and clarinet to F.

Specific Requirements/Considerations: Slow sustained playing is called for.

Instructional Concepts/Skills: Chorale style, phrasing, tuning, legato trombone playing, and balanced blend are all a part of this piece. There are entrances on the second half of the beat and some ties.

General Comments: Although this chorale is very easy, it has so much to offer musically that even advanced groups can learn from it. It can be used with honor groups to get them to listen to and follow a rubato beat.

—Submitted by Dixie Detgen

Title: Starship One
Level/Grade: 1
Composer/Arranger: Jay Chattaway
Publisher: William Allen
Classification: Contemporary
Duration: 2:00

Instrumentation: Standard with good percussion

Specific Requirements/Considerations: No problems

Instructional Concepts/Skills: Articulation; tuning/sonority; contrast/scoring

General Comments: Excellent parts for all instruments; wonderful sonorities; good percussion parts; exciting and fun to perform

—*Submitted by Ted Hadley*

Title: The Water Is Wide
Level/Grade: 1
Composer/Arranger: Arr. Julie Griffin
Publisher: Musicworks
Classification: Folk
Duration: 2:30

Instrumentation: Standard; section solos

Specific Requirements/Considerations: No problems

Instructional Concepts/Skills: Expressive/lyric/line concepts; musically challenging; modulation; contrast/balance

General Comments: Beautiful melody; well arranged; an excellent Grade 1 teaching piece

—*Submitted by Ted Hadley*

Title: Fanfare and Fugue
Level/Grade: 1¹/₂
Composer/Arranger: Ann McGinty
Publisher: Hal Leonard
Classification: Fanfare and fugue
Duration: 2:00

Instrumentation: Instruments are in a comfortable range for young players.

Specific Requirements/Considerations: Parts are doubled in the fugue section. This piece is very good for ear training and for teaching balance.

Instructional Concepts/Skills: An excellent piece for teaching fugue form—the fugue melody (statement) is well written. Balance and intonation are a must.

General Comments: McGinty voices the fugue very musically, and her instrumentation allows bands to perform this successfully. Bands without full instrumentation can also perform this piece effectively.

—*Submitted by Nancy Sieloff-Ruebke*

Title: Little Jazz Suite

Level/Grade: 1¹/₂

Composer/Arranger: Deane Bottorf

Publisher: Warner Bros. Publications

Classification: Three-part suite:
1. Weirdsville
2. Bionic Blues
3. Little Black Book

Duration: 6:00 (without extended improvisation)

Instrumentation: Optional electric bass and guitar parts and piano part

Specific Requirements/Considerations: Each individual part has "usable improvisatory pitches." The piece offers students a chance to add a drum set, piano, guitar, and electric bass (or acoustic) to the band.

Instructional Concepts/Skills: This is a piece for teaching jazz styles and introducing improvisation. Notes that "sound good" with the harmony are provided in the band parts, thus giving inventive, creative students fundamental pitches/sounds to assist in the development of improvisational skills.

General Comments: An entertaining concert piece that can feature "soloists."

—*Submitted by Ken Feneley*

Title: Prehistoric Suite

Level/Grade: 1$^1/_2$

Composer/Arranger: Paul Jennings

Publisher: Jenson

Classification: Four-part suite:

        1. Stegosaurus—The Gladiator

        2. Brontosaurus—Gentle Giant

        3. Pterodactyls—Graceful Giants of the Sky

        4. The Battle—Tyrannosaurs and Triceratops

Duration: 6:00

Instrumentation: A gong is called for. Solid percussion playing is crucial.

Specific Requirements/Considerations: Various sections are exposed.

Instructional Concepts/Skills: Music styles from heavy marcato to delicate legato are needed. Imaginatively depicting the various animals of each movement in a musical manner is challenging but rewarding to the students.

General Comments: Students find this music extremely interesting, thus making it a real pleasure to teach. This is terrific music for the very young band.

—Submitted by Ken Feneley

Title: Tall Cedars Concert March
Level/Grade: 1¹/2
Composer/Arranger: Eric Osterling
Publisher: Carl Fischer
Classification: March
Duration: 2:30

Instrumentation: Standard; doubling of parts

Specific Requirements/Considerations: Low brass section solo (exposed section, trio); no individual solos; no technical problems; a range that is within junior high/middle school level of playing

Instructional Concepts/Skills: This piece serves as a good example of the basic band march. It offers students experience with two different key signatures: Concert E-flat and Concert B-flat. It is filled with numerous articulations: accents (marcato), staccato, and slurs. The dynamic range includes p to ff. The melodic line is often doubled, allowing students to focus on balance and blend of the ensemble.

General Comments: This is a good piece for junior high/middle-level bands as it is scored within a reasonable playing range. It demands observation of articulations and dynamics and works well for this age group. Students enjoy this piece as do audiences.

—*Submitted by T. Broyles-Brouillard*

Title: Winchester March
Level/Grade: 1 ¹/₂
Composer/Arranger: John Edmondson
Publisher: Charles Hansen (recently reissued by Queenwood)
Classification: March
Duration: 2:00

Instrumentation: This is a march that a Class C or D band can play. The instrumentation and range are very playable for young students.

Specific Requirements/Considerations: Exposed sections occur in the Grandioso section with the woodwinds. Percussionists must be above the beginner level with crash cymbal solos. There are no extreme ranges.

Instructional Concepts/Skills: This is an excellent march to teach march style. There are many dynamic contrasts, good balance is vital, and separation is a must. The Grandioso section of the march teaches the students a slow strong march style with an accelerando to take the band back to an "a tempo" section. It is an unusual march for a young band as the tempo change in the Grandioso is a challenge.

General Comments: The challenge of this composition is being able to perform a march that includes both a style and tempo change. It is a very good piece of music for teaching new concepts to the young player. It is a good festival/concert march for young bands.

—*Submitted by Nancy Sieloff-Ruebke*

Level 2–2½

Title: Allegro and Dance
Level/Grade: 2
Composer/Arranger: Mozart/Cacavas
Publisher: Theodore Presser
Classification: Two-part transcription
Duration: 3:00

Instrumentation: Full instrumentation is needed for this composition. (It would be very difficult to try to change the instrumentation, as it loses quality.)

Specific Requirements/Considerations: All sections must have strong technical ability. Full ensemble is generally used, but the director must decide if the full section is used because of the difficulty involved.

Instructional Concepts/Skills: The lightness and clarity of the musical line is the most difficult concept to teach. The piece encompasses two works, and the concepts in this classical literature are worth the struggle to teach the basics.

General Comments: This composition gives the teacher an opportunity to expose his or her students to classical literature. The arrangement is skillfully done. Once the students grasp the concepts of this Mozart work, they really enjoy it. It is a great contest/festival number.

—*Submitted by Nancy Sieloff-Ruebke*

Title: La Banda Nascente
Level/Grade: 2
Composer/Arranger: Sbraccia/Fennell
Publisher: Kjos
Classification: March (Italian)
Duration: 2:00

Instrumentation: Standard with piccolo, E-flat clarinet, E-flat contrabass clarinet, string bass, and timpani

Specific Requirements/Considerations: This piece is nicely balanced between melody, countermelody, and harmonic rhythm. There are no awkward or unreachable demands.

Instructional Concepts/Skills: This piece has a minor tonality, which is common in Italian marches. It was written in the early 1900s by one of the many Italian composers who came to the U.S. and began to write for the many adult bands of the era. It calls for balance, blend, melody, and countermelody. It is superbly scored and easy to teach.

General Comments: This fine march is really only a Grade 2 or 2½ at best, yet it makes a finely tuned ensemble sound like a mature band. It flows and is extremely playable. It forces the students to listen to the wonderful things going on around them.

—Submitted by David Reul

Title: Belle Qui Tiens Ma Vie
Level/Grade: 2
Composer/Arranger: Arbeau/Margolis
Publisher: Manhattan Beach
Classification: Concert piece
Duration: 2:45

Instrumentation: Standard with piccolo and E-flat clarinet, E-flat contrabass clarinet; 1, 2 horns

Specific Requirements/Considerations: There are no special requirements, other than superb musicianship required to re-create the piece in its original intent.

Instructional Concepts/Skills: Margolis has done a great service with his extensive notes about the music. Block scoring is important as well as contrasting dynamics. For balance and blend, the parts must not be heavy and ponderous. The teacher can touch on harmonic analysis and discuss the piece's sensitivity and beauty through simplicity.

General Comments: There are superb historical and biographical notes. This simple period piece is a delight to truly "discover," but it needs good teaching to do just that. It's a real gem.

—Submitted by David Reul

Title: Castlebrook: Overture
Level/Grade: 2
Composer/Arranger: Claude T. Smith
Publisher: Jenson
Classification: Overture
Duration: 2:40

Instrumentation: Clarinet has 3-way division. Trumpet and trombone have 2-way division. Range is high B for clarinet and high E (on the staff) for trumpet.

Specific Requirements/Considerations: Melody moves from tutti high instruments to tutti low instruments. The piece has a short bell solo. It also has a few exposed horn measures, but they are cued if necessary.

Instructional Concepts/Skills: Music is in the key of Concert F throughout, but in typical Claude T. Smith style, the meter change is there (from 4/4 to 3/8 to 4/4). It's in variation form. There are lots of tied notes and style changes.

General Comments: This piece has much to teach students. There is no end to the rehearsal time the teacher could spend digging out the details. The melody moves from section to section so there are lots of balance and blend concepts to teach. There are lots of unisons for tuning.

—Submitted by Dixie Detgen

Title: Chichester Overture
Level/Grade: 2
Composer/Arranger: John O'Reilly
Publisher: Queenwood
Classification: Concert overture
Duration: 3:00

Instrumentation: No instrumentation problems exist. Overall range is not a problem and no unusual combinations exist.

Specific Requirements/Considerations: Strong sections are necessary—trumpets are exposed at the beginning. Range for instruments is not difficult.

Instructional Concepts/Skills: The students must be very secure in the dotted eighth and sixteenth note pattern throughout this piece. Syncopation concepts must be taught to make this composition successful.

General Comments: This composition is a pleasant piece for audience listening. The fanfare beginning is very skillfully written, and the students enjoy performing this composition. It is a good contest/festival composition.

—*Submitted by Nancy Sieloff-Ruebke*

Title: Chorale and Fugue in F Major
Level/Grade: 2
Composer/Arranger: Bach/Daehn
Publisher: Daehn Publishing
Classification: Chorale and fugue
Duration: 3:00

Instrumentation: Timpani is optional; bells and chime are also optional. Instrumentation is standard, plus piccolo; E-flat clarinet; 1, 2 horns; and 1, 2, 3 trombones.

Specific Requirements/Considerations: Fugue parts are nicely doubled but soli in nature.

Instructional Concepts/Skills: Chorale and fugue concepts can be discussed. Balance and blend are essential. Bach wrote these two works during his Weimar period. They can be used to teach harmony, counterpoint, and phrasing (musical sentences and structure).

General Comments: This is a gem of a chorale and fugue. Although reachable for Grade 2, it still needs that mature teaching approach to make it come alive as a work of art, which it certainly is.

—*Submitted by David Reul*

Title: Command March
Level/Grade: 2
Composer/Arranger: John Edmondson
Publisher: Barnhouse
Classification: March
Duration: 1:45

Instrumentation: No unusual combinations or instruments are needed.

Specific Requirements/Considerations: This piece begins with a percussion ensemble. It also has an interesting variation for flute in the Grandioso section.

Instructional Concepts/Skills: This piece, in the keys of G minor and C minor, can be used to introduce and discuss minor tonality.

General Comments: This is an excellent march for class D or C junior high/middle school band. It has great tone colors and a wide dynamic range.

—Submitted by William Sutherland

Title: Early English Suite
Level/Grade: 2
Composer/Arranger: Duncombe/Finlayson
Publisher: Boosey and Hawkes
Classification: Suite
Duration: 8:00

Instrumentation: Instrumentation calls for full band, and the piece is most effectively performed with full band. Overall range is for the medium to advanced middle school/junior high student. There are no unusual combinations.

Specific Requirements/Considerations: The second and third movements have exposed woodwind sections. The bass clarinet plays a major role in the success of these movements. The fourth movement provides a challenge to the trumpets and woodwinds.

Instructional Concepts/Skills: This composition exposes students to 3/4 and 6/8 classical styles. It is not demanding for the percussion section. Balance and blend is a must to perform the composition successfully. Students can learn style and characteristics of early English dance suites.

General Comments: This composition is useful for teaching light, sensitive, musical playing. It provides training in 6/8 and 3/4 rhythms. It is a great festival/contest selection and is interesting for both student and audience.

—Submitted by Nancy Sieloff-Ruebke

Title: Festivity
Level/Grade: 2
Composer/Arranger: John Kinyon
Publisher: Alfred
Classification: Concert overture
Duration: 3:20

Instrumentation: The scoring is very safe for the young band and there are no instrumentation problems—overall range is fine.

Specific Requirements/Considerations: Technical problems exist in the syncopated dance rhythms.

Instructional Concepts/Skills: The skills taught are ABA form and syncopation (rhythm). The syncopation is difficult at first and becomes a challenge to the students.

General Comments: The students like this piece once it is learned. The syncopated Latin dance style is fun for performers and audience. It is a good selection for any type of performance.

—Submitted by Nancy Sieloff-Ruebke

Title: The Headless Horseman
Level/Grade: 2
Composer/Arranger: Timothy Broege
Publisher: Manhattan Beach
Classification: Program music
Duration: 2:00

Instrumentation: Standard instrumentation

Specific Requirements/Considerations: This piece has creative percussion parts. It has trombone glissandos in the range of B-flat to low E-flat. It has tutti soli sections for trombone, baritone, and tuba.

Instructional Concepts/Skills: This is a creative piece that introduces students to 6/4 meter, staccatos, slurs, accented staccatos, and several dynamic contrasts from *p* to *ff*. This composition is unique as it is creatively written and depicts the famous ride of Washington Irving's "Headless Horseman." The percussion parts include snare, bells, crash cymbal, suspended cymbal, woodblock, and bass drum. The low brass section will discover glissandos.

General Comments: The music of Timothy Broege is filled with creative ideas and offers students a challenge that is truly rewarding. This piece is enjoyed by both those who play it and those who listen to it (it is extremely programmatic).

—Submitted by T. Broyles-Brouillard

Title: Joyous Episode
Level/Grade: 2
Composer/Arranger: David Gorham
Publisher: Wingert-Jones
Classification: Overture
Duration: 3:30

Instrumentation: Clarinet, trumpet, and trombone have 2-way division. The range is to high F for both clarinet and trumpet.

Specific Requirements/Considerations: There are flute and trumpet soli sections. This piece uses a rhythm of an eighth note and two sixteenth notes in the fast movement. There are some difficult articulations.

Instructional Concepts/Skills: The time signature changes three times. There are many style changes and opportunities to teach phrasing. Exposed parts are soli so there is security while teaching independence. Articulations have to be checked to keep a clean sound. The usual dynamic shifts are there. The piece has a D.S. al coda.

General Comments: This music has the feel of a more difficult piece, utilizing the same concepts, yet it is very playable.

—Submitted by Dixie Detgen

Title: The King's Musicke
Level/Grade: 2
Composer/Arranger: Arr. Philip Gordon
Publisher: Boosey and Hawkes
Classification: Suite of Baroque dances
Duration: 3:00

Instrumentation: Standard instrumentation—the range is Concert low A to Concert high F.

Specific Requirements/Considerations: There are three movements: I. Minuet—trumpet solo; II. Sarabande—oboe or clarinet I solo; and III. March.

Instructional Concepts/Skills: This work represents a three-movement composition created using melodious airs written by Jeremiah Clarke, William Croft, and Francis Piggot (Baroque composers). When teaching this piece, the teacher can work on the style of Baroque music, proper balance/blend of the ensemble, and numerous musical terms: allegretto, tutti, andante, rallentando, diminuendo, and allargando. This short piece allows for solo playing in addition to some very nice full ensemble playing.

General Comments: This work is scored well for young bands, especially junior high/middle school bands. It teaches students about musical terms, solo playing, and Baroque music. Students really enjoy this piece.

—Submitted by T. Broyles-Brouillard

Title: Korean Folk Rhapsody
Level/Grade: 2
Composer/Arranger: Jim Curnow
Publisher: Jenson
Classification: Rhapsody
Duration: 4:50

Instrumentation: Standard with nice percussion

Specific Requirements/Considerations: Several section solos with optional solos

Instructional Concepts/Skills: This piece can be used to teach balance/blend, line concepts, expressive playing, and coordination of diverse musical elements.

General Comments: This piece has some lovely sounds and sonorities. It is a good introduction to Korean folk melody concepts. It is an excellent multicultural folk medley for young bands.

—Submitted by Ted Hadley

Title: Modal Song and Dance
Level/Grade: 2
Composer/Arranger: Elliot Del Borgo
Publisher: William Allen
Classification: Overture
Duration: 2:48

Instrumentation: Clarinet and trumpet have 2-way division. Trombone is unison as are alto saxophone and horns. Range is to high E for both clarinet and trumpet.

Specific Requirements/Considerations: This piece has a very easy percussion soli part. It has some tricky entrances.

Instructional Concepts/Skills: The "Modal Song" is slow so lots of phrasing, dynamics, and balance is needed. The "Dance" is fast and has several tricky, exposed entrances that teach independent playing. The piece provides an opportunity to discuss modal music.

General Comments: This piece is very appropriate for festivals or contests because there is so much teaching material and it is such a good contrasting piece to program.

—Submitted by Dixie Detgen

Title: Nathan Hale Trilogy
Level/Grade: 2
Composer/Arranger: James Curnow
Publisher: Hal Leonard
Classification: Trilogy
Duration: 6:00

Instrumentation: No unusual instruments or combinations

Specific Requirements/Considerations: No extreme technical problems

Instructional Concepts/Skills: There are three contrasting movements. The "intrada" has excellent rhythmic drive that is an interesting concept to show students. The "intermezzo," with its beautiful melodic line, is wonderful for teaching phrasing. The "finale" has some new and interesting rhythms to teach students.

General Comments: This is an excellent teaching piece. It is very popular with both students and audiences.

—*Submitted by William Sutherland*

Title: Portrait of a Clown
Level/Grade: 2
Composer/Arranger: Frank Tichelli
Publisher: Manhattan Beach
Classification: Descriptive fantasy
Duration: 2:30

Instrumentation: There is an absence of "block scoring." Instruments are nicely doubled for a band that lacks low reed and brass.

Specific Requirements/Considerations: There are no extreme challenges.

Instructional Concepts/Skills: The form is ABA, plus an 8-bar introduction and coda. The center section is in the Lydian mode. The piece has countermelody and inversion. Articulations include staccato, legato, and accents.

General Comments: This is a work of art. The scoring is open, requiring students to listen. The melody is catchy and requires the best from everyone, yet it is very appealing to the middle-level student. Superb program notes are provided by the composer. The piece is simple, yet so delicately musical—a masterpiece for a good teacher.

—Submitted by David Reul

Title: Sounds of Sousa
Level/Grade: 2
Composer/Arranger: Sousa/Ployhar
Publisher: Warner Bros. Publications
Classification: March
Duration: 3:30

Instrumentation: There is no unusual instrumentation, and the range for individual sections is not demanding.

Specific Requirements/Considerations: Trumpets, percussion, and trombones are exposed. The time signature moves from cut time to 6/8 to cut time. This is a challenge for young bands.

Instructional Concepts/Skills: The skills and concepts taught in this piece are teaching cut-time and 6/8. The style of a Sousa march is a basic concept all students should be exposed to during their musical education. The teaching of dynamics, articulations, and correct percussion techniques is integral to this piece.

General Comments: This is a great introduction to three Sousa marches. It is a real crowd pleaser and a must for the junior high/middle school band director who wants to introduce Sousa to his or her students.

—Submitted by Nancy Sieloff-Ruebke

Title: Suite in Minor Mode
Level/Grade: 2
Composer/Arranger: Kabalevsky/Siekman-Oliver
Publisher: MCA Music
Classification: Suite: three movements
Duration: 4:00

Instrumentation: This piece has standard instrumentation. The range is from Concert low A-flat to Concert high F.

Specific Requirements/Considerations: There are no specified solos. Some beautiful clarinet, trumpet, and trombone tutti sections appear in Movement II ("A Little Song").

Instructional Concepts/Skills: This is a great teaching piece for basic rhythmic concepts. Movement I is filled with eighth note patterns and eighth rests. Movement II is a good example of legato style of playing. This movement has several tutti soli sections; the harmonies are quite nice. Movement III challenges students by calling for the dotted eighth and sixteenth note pattern, afterbeats, slurs, and a tempo indicated at "quarter note = 138."

General Comments: Students enjoy the melodic material within this composition. Although Movement II is slow, students begin to discover the beautiful harmonies and their relationship to the melody. Movement III is a challenging song, one that students really enjoy.

—*Submitted by T. Broyles-Brouillard*

Title: Triumphant Festival
Level/Grade: 2
Composer/Arranger: Handel/Kinyon
Publisher: Alfred
Classification: Transcription
Duration: 2:00

Instrumentation: Standard

Specific Requirements/Considerations: Brass is featured prominently, but there are quality parts for all instruments.

Instructional Concepts/Skills: This piece calls for contrasting band choirs. It can be used to teach articulation, style, and dynamics.

General Comments: This is a great introduction to Baroque music. It is fun to play and the audience likes it, too. It sounds genuine in cut time but is also effective at a slower tempo.

—Submitted by Ted Hadley

Title: Vantage Overture
Level/Grade: 2
Composer/Arranger: Lloyd Conley
Publisher: Columbia Pictures Publishing
Classification: Overture
Duration: 3:30

Instrumentation: Percussionists need a vibra-slap and tom-tom to complement the usual percussion needs of snare, bass drum, suspended cymbal, and timpani.

Specific Requirements/Considerations: A strong percussion section along with antiphonal section work is required in this work.

Instructional Concepts/Skills: All rhythms and ranges are very playable in this piece. However, executing section and part passages makes this piece more challenging than it appears. Still, the results are worth the effort.

General Comments: This is exciting music, and it is interesting for the player and listener. It is wonderful material for the developing band.

—Submitted by Ken Feneley

Title: Air de Sarabande
Level/Grade: 2½
Composer/Arranger: Handel/Reed
Publisher: Hal Leonard
Classification: Air
Duration: 2:50

Instrumentation: This piece has standard instrumentation. The percussion parts are for timpani only. The range is from Concert low A-flat to Concert high E-flat.

Specific Requirements/Considerations: This composition can be performed with the oboe playing the solo in measures 1 to 10 and 19 to 31.

Instructional Concepts/Skills: This piece works well for teaching the legato style of playing, balance, blend, independence of musical line, phrasing, and intonation. Rhythmically, there are several challenges within this work including dotted quarter and eighth note patterns, ties over the bar line, and dotted eighth and sixteenth note patterns. When using this piece as a solo work for oboe, the teacher can help students discover the concertino style of playing. At the junior high/middle school level, students should be exposed to this form of music making.

General Comments: "Air de Sarabande" is simply a beautiful arrangement scored very nicely by Alfred Reed. Performance of this piece demands a legato style of playing, something all middle school and high school musicians need constant exposure to.

—Submitted by T. Broyles-Brouillard

Title: Beethoven's Four Dances
Level/Grade: 2½
Composer/Arranger: Beethoven/Rizzo
Publisher: Bourne
Classification: Dances
Duration: 6:00

Instrumentation: Full instrumentation is necessary. Overall range for sections is above average for junior high/middle school students.

Specific Requirements/Considerations: Soloists are oboe, alto saxophone, French horn, and trumpet. Technical problems exist with developing clean articulation and lightness.

Instructional Concepts/Skills: Students can learn the classical style, lightness in technique, and style changes. Students must play confidently and be independently secure. When this piece is performed successfully, the students grow musically.

General Comments: This composition presents a real challenge to the students, teaches good classical literature techniques, and is excellent for musical training. This piece is not often performed, yet it is one of the best classical pieces for young players. It is a must for young players performing at an advanced level.

—Submitted by Nancy Sieloff-Ruebke

Title: Fanfare Prelude on "Ode to Joy"
Level/Grade: 2½
Composer/Arranger: Beethoven/Curnow
Publisher: Jenson
Classification: Fanfare prelude
Duration: 2:55

Instrumentation: Clarinet and trumpet have a 3-way division. Trombone has a 2-way division. Clarinet range is to high C, and trumpet range is to high G. Trombone range is to high F. Keys are Concert F to Concert B-flat. There is no time change.

Specific Requirements/Considerations: The first 8 bars are the most difficult. Once they are learned, the arrangement is very playable.

Instructional Concepts/Skills: The piece has a nice mallet part, limited trills, varied styles from marcato to sostenuto, brass choir, and woodwind choir. The piece provides an opportunity to discuss Beethoven and the Ninth Symphony. The low brass have to extend their range for this arrangement.

General Comments: There is a lot of teaching material in this work. It can be used with a second group, although there is a difficult introduction. The students really enjoy the piece.

—*Submitted by Dixie Detgen*

Title: Gentlemen's Agreement
Level/Grade: 2½
Composer/Arranger: Leland Forsblad
Publisher: Heritage
Classification: Concert march
Duration: 3:00

Instrumentation: Clarinet, trumpet, and trombone all have 2-way division. The range is clarinet to high A and trumpet to high F.

Specific Requirements/Considerations: This piece has some soli work for clarinet and alto saxophone and a nice low woodwind/brass part in the break strain. It has a D.S. al fine with repeat.

Instructional Concepts/Skills: This piece calls for march style, syncopation, cut time, and the key of Concert E-flat. There is a nice countermelody in the ending strain.

General Comments: This march is very interesting and teaches nearly every march concept there is. It's quite long with all the repeats, so it can be an endurance test. It is a good festival/contest march.

—Submitted by Dixie Detgen

Title: Greensleeves
Level/Grade: 2½
Composer/Arranger: arr. Alfred Reed
Publisher: Hansen
Classification: Folk song
Duration: 3:00

Instrumentation: This piece has standard instrumentation with little percussion emphasis. It has moderate ranges.

Specific Requirements/Considerations: There is dependence on soli scoring in the woodwinds, and the piece has a short oboe solo.

Instructional Concepts/Skills: This piece calls for intuitive sensitivity—the music is very much alive. There are no rote rhythms. The student is forced to listen and get involved musically. There is dynamic contrast. Breath support is essential to timing and phrasing.

General Comments: This piece calls for interdependence of the entire woodwind section. The music is beautifully scored and provides a rich harmonic development of the basic theme. It is a work of art. Adolescents know the tune and are challenged by the setting.

—Submitted by David Reul

Title: Invocation and Jubiloso
Level/Grade: 2½
Composer/Arranger: Claude T. Smith
Publisher: Jenson
Classification: Overture
Duration: 2:00

Instrumentation: Clarinet has 3-way division. Trumpet has 2-way division. Clarinet range is to high B. Trumpet range is to E.

Specific Requirements/Considerations: This piece has a very short trombone solo, exposed percussion tutti parts, and several awkward trombone slurs.

Instructional Concepts/Skills: This piece has many dynamic contrasts, mixed meter, and a slow, sustained style that is contrasted with a very rhythmic section. Other features include syncopation, a D.S. al coda, and material that needs to be balanced.

General Comments: This piece has many concepts to teach. It is in a minor key and is a great contrasting piece for festival or contest. The invocation is full of opportunities for teaching phrasing and nuance in playing.

—Submitted by Dixie Detgen

Title: Joyant Winds
Level/Grade: 2½
Composer/Arranger: Ed Huckeby
Publisher: Barnhouse
Classification: Overture
Duration: 3:20

Instrumentation: Clarinet, trumpet, and trombone all have 2-way division. Range is to high G for both clarinet and trumpet.

Specific Requirements/Considerations: There are several clarinet soli parts.

Instructional Concepts/Skills: The key of Concert F changes to the key of B-flat. There is a meter change from 4/4 to 6/8 and then back to 4/4. There are also several 3/4 sections. The piece calls for a dotted eighth and sixteenth note rhythm plus syncopation. There is a very musical slow section, with a D.S. al coda. Several woodwind trills and varying styles are called for.

General Comments: The mixed meter is interesting. The piece has a great deal to offer both as a teaching piece and as a way to show off a group for festival or contest. There's a lot to dig out and rehearse in this piece.

—Submitted by Dixie Detgen

Title: Kentucky 1800
Level/Grade: 2½
Composer/Arranger: Clare Grundman
Publisher: Boosey and Hawkes
Classification: Overture
Duration: 3:30

Instrumentation: Standard instrumentation—the range is from low B-flat to high G.

Specific Requirements/Considerations: There is a brief trumpet solo, which is three measures long. The key changes include B-flat, A-flat, and E-flat. There is chromaticism throughout.

Instructional Concepts/Skills: Grundman employs numerous dynamics, articulations, and key changes in addition to a variety of rhythmic patterns (up through dotted eighth and sixteenth note patterns). All of these ideas work well with junior high/middle school musicians. Grundman's scoring of this piece provides all instruments with various melodic parts. This is an effective piece for the teaching of balance and blend within the ensemble.

General Comments: Students enjoy "Kentucky 1800" and its melodies, harmonies, and challenging rhythmic patterns. There is a great deal of music in this piece.

—Submitted by T. Broyles-Brouillard

Title: Little Suite for Band
Level/Grade: 2½
Composer/Arranger: Clare Grundman
Publisher: Boosey and Hawkes
Classification: Suite
Duration: 3:30

Instrumentation: Instrumentation is standard, with piccolo and E-flat clarinet. Ranges are at intermediate level.

Specific Requirements/Considerations: Scalewise runs, 7 on 1 beat (a "sweep"), are in the woodwinds.

Instructional Concepts/Skills: This piece can be used to teach the suite. It has three beautifully contrasting sections, which are very musical. The piece calls for articulation (marcato, accents, staccato, legato), balance, and blend.

General Comments: A superb set of contrasting styles that are in and of themselves fine cameos. Put together, they make an interesting and enjoyable performance piece. The last movement is a delight to the adolescent musician. Its driving rhythm is totally engrossing, but it still requires musicianship (not rote playing) as a catalyst for performance.

—Submitted by David Reul

Title: Rhythm Machine
Level/Grade: 2½
Composer/Arranger: Timothy Broege
Publisher: Bourne
Classification: Rondo
Duration: 3:20

Instrumentation: The instrumentation is standard with piccolo; E-flat clarinet (no contrabass clarinet); 1, 2 horn; 1, 2, 3 cornet; and 1, 2 trombone.

Specific Requirements/Considerations: This piece has many soli clarinet and flute passages and a 16-bar trumpet solo (to high G on the staff). The first clarinets must be able to play C in the bass clef in tune.

Instructional Concepts/Skills: Rondo form: easy to see and hear, yet totally creative so that the form is not monotonous. Rhythm: dotted eighth and sixteenth note patterns; triplets. Articulation: accents on off-beats. Tuning: critical, especially for flute and clarinet. Creativity: a masterpiece for middle-level bands; full of joy.

General Comments: One of Broege's all-time greats. Totally creative, yet musically and harmonically "clear." Three major styles—all clever and fun—and great fun in the hands of a good teacher.

—Submitted by David Reul

Title: Saratoga March
Level/Grade: 2½
Composer/Arranger: Jerry Nowak
Publisher: Kendor Music
Classification: March
Duration: 2:30

Instrumentation: No unusual instruments are needed—standard instrumentation. The range is normal for this level of difficulty

Specific Requirements/Considerations: This piece is not difficult technically, but it has many musical opportunities.

Instructional Concepts/Skills: This piece is in a march style. It is in the keys of Concert E-flat and Concert B-flat. It is an excellent piece for teaching syncopation.

General Comments: This is an excellent march for young bands. It can be used to reinforce march form and syncopation.

—Submitted by William Sutherland

Title: Shilo Canyon Fantasy
Level/Grade: 2½
Composer/Arranger: Douglas Akey
Publisher: Queenwood
Classification: Fantasy
Duration: 6:30

Instrumentation: Full instrumentation is necessary. Oboe, bassoon, and French horn play major parts in this composition. The overall range of the instruments is above average for junior high/middle school students.

Specific Requirements/Considerations: Must have strong individual players—there are baritone, French horn, alto saxophone, and percussion solos. Woodwind players must have command of their instruments technically.

Instructional Concepts/Skills: This piece of music is wonderful for teaching style changes. It starts with a powerful introduction, followed by a snare solo to introduce a second section. Students must learn to play legato and staccato and to handle powerful tutti sections and a light style. This piece has every imaginable style.

General Comments: This is a superbly scored composition. It is an excellent contest composition. The students love playing it, and it is a really pleasant composition for the listener. This composition keeps the percussion section very active.

—Submitted by Nancy Sieloff-Ruebke

Title: Suite for Winds and Percussion
Level/Grade: 2½
Composer/Arranger: Timothy Broege
Publisher: Hal Leonard
Classification: Suite: three movements
Duration: 4:00

Instrumentation: The range is from Concert low G to Concert high F.

Specific Requirements/Considerations: Percussion parts are challenging and creatively composed. Movement II has beautiful harmonies and tutti soli sections.

Instructional Concepts/Skills: Movement I includes meter changes, 4/4 to 3/4, and so forth. This must reinforce articulations: accent, staccato, and so forth. It demands various dynamic contrasts, ranging from *p* to *ff*. Movement II is a beautiful piece with tutti soli baritones. The harmony is also quite nice. Movement III has meter changes from 2/2 to 3/2, and so forth. This movement is challenging in that it demands several different articulations, dynamics, and challenging percussion parts.

General Comments: This piece has always been a favorite of middle school students. It is creative, challenging, and most enjoyable to play. Audiences also love this piece. It includes some interesting percussion parts.

—*Submitted by T. Broyles-Brouillard*

Title: A Tallis Prelude
Level/Grade: 2½
Composer/Arranger: Douglas Akey
Publisher: Queenwood
Classification: Hymn fantasy
Duration: 3:30

Instrumentation: Standard: piccolo (no E-flat clarinet); 1, 2 horns; 1, 2, 3 trombones; extensive percussion, including mallets

Specific Requirements/Considerations: Hemiola rhythm in 6/8 compound; easy to learn; challenging mallet work

Instructional Concepts/Skills: Historical: Thomas Tallis, sixteenth-century composer, wrote some of the earliest hymns in homophonic idiom. Tonality: Phrygian mode— haunting quality; relative major key for all "non-theme" inventions. Rhythm: 6/8 compound; mixed meter; interesting 6/8, 2/4, 3/4 driving percussive rhythms.

General Comments: A gem of a piece in its ability to first set the Tallis chorale for the listener and then, in a contrasting section, build a fantasy that almost disguises the chorale theme. Very creative writing.

—Submitted by David Reul

Title: A Thousand Hills Overture
Level/Grade: 2½
Composer/Arranger: Claude T. Smith
Publisher: Jenson
Classification: Overture
Duration: 5:00

Instrumentation: Standard

Specific Requirements/Considerations: Section solos

Instructional Concepts/Skills: Introduction to changing and mixed meters; articulation; contrasting expressive middle section

General Comments: Exciting; fun parts for all; "real" band music

—Submitted by Ted Hadley

Title: Three Folk Tunes
Level/Grade: 2½
Composer/Arranger: Holst/Curnow
Publisher: Jenson
Classification: March
Duration: 1:55

Instrumentation: Standard (no E-flat clarinet, E-flat contrabass clarinet); moderate range—no surprises

Specific Requirements/Considerations: No significant problems

Instructional Concepts/Skills: Historical context: first folk tune is famous march from *Suite in E-flat* by Holst in its original form. The piece calls for articulation (staccato), dynamic contrast, and the English march style.

General Comments: This is a great middle-level piece that is preparatory for the standard suite in E-flat that most students get in high school. Also, it's a nice musical Grade 2 selection. It's easy to learn and fun to perform.

—Submitted by David Reul

Title: Three Kentucky Sketches
Level/Grade: 2½
Composer/Arranger: John O'Reilly
Publisher: Queenwood
Classification: Suite
Duration: 6:00

Instrumentation: Full instrumentation is necessary. No unusual combinations; no particular range problems.

Specific Requirements/Considerations: No extreme ranges exist. Technical problems exist in syncopated rhythms. Sections are usually doubled, so no exposed sections exist.

Instructional Concepts/Skills: Concepts taught in this selection are unison playing with full band. This creates intonation problems that must be concentrated on for a successful performance. Students can learn three different styles of music in this composition.

General Comments: This composition is a cleverly written piece with some unique musical styles—a very pleasant piece for the audience. The students enjoy performing and learning this piece. It is an excellent contest/festival number.

—*Submitted by Nancy Sieloff-Ruebke*

Title: Yorkshire Ballad
Level/Grade: 2½
Composer/Arranger: James Barnes
Publisher: Southern Music Company
Classification: Ballad
Duration: 3:40

Instrumentation: The instrumentation is standard. The range is from Concert low B-flat to Concert high E-flat.

Specific Requirements/Considerations: The technical difficulties within this work include challenging French horn parts and rhythmic patterns tied over the bar line. This piece requires basic rhythmic skill development of each player.

Instructional Concepts/Skills: This beautiful composition demands that students play expressively using a legato style of playing. This work offers two key signatures: Concert B-flat and Concert E-flat. Students are required to incorporate numerous dynamic changes and crescendo/decrescendos in addition to observing slurs and ties. Barnes includes several musical terms in his score (students' parts), teaching the players about this language (e.g., tranquillo, dim. poco a poco, morendo al niente).

General Comments: "Yorkshire Ballad" is scored beautifully for wind band and includes musical lines that flow and are expressive. This work demands that musicians play sustained lines, musical phrases, and numerous dynamics. It is challenging rhythmically for there are numerous ties/slurs across the bar line.

—*Submitted by T. Broyles-Brouillard*

Level 3–3½

Title: Air for Band
Level/Grade: 3
Composer/Arranger: Frank Erickson
Publisher: Bourne
Classification: Air
Duration: 3:00 to 3:30

Instrumentation: Standard instrumentation; range: Concert low B-flat to Concert high E-flat

Instructional Concepts/Skills: This is an effective piece for teaching students the legato style of playing. This composition includes challenging parts that often have rhythmic patterns tied over the bar line. This work demands observation of dynamics and slurred passages. A good piece for teaching balance, blend, intonation, phrasing.

General Comments: This is a classic piece for any band.

—Submitted by T. Broyles-Brouillard

Title: Air for Winds
Level/Grade: 3
Composer/Arranger: Melvin Shelton
Publisher: Ludwig
Classification: Air
Duration: 3:00

Instrumentation: Standard

Specific Requirements/Considerations: A few optional solos

Instructional Concepts/Skills: Tuning, line concepts, breath control, lyric playing

General Comments: This piece has a beautiful melody and nice scoring. It is useable as a holiday concert selection.

—Submitted by Ted Hadley

Title: Carlyle Trilogy
Level/Grade: 3
Composer/Arranger: Frank J. Halferty
Publisher: Alfred
Classification: Three-movement trilogy
Duration: 4:15

Instrumentation: Movement II: wind chimes in percussion

Specific Requirements/Considerations: Movement I has trombones to high F and trumpets to high G. Movements II and III have nice horn parts.

Instructional Concepts/Skills: This piece can be used to teach contrasting styles. Movement I ("The Bridge") is in 3/2 but has a natural feel. Movement II ("Winter Morning") has a nice low clarinet and horn melody. Movement III ("Lake Festival") presents a good opportunity to teach 6/8 march style.

General Comments: This is an excellent teaching piece for advanced middle school/junior high band. It has nice contrasting styles and a lot of music to be made.

—Submitted by William Sutherland

Title: Celebrated Air
Level/Grade: 3
Composer/Arranger: Bach/Walters
Publisher: Rubank
Classification: Transcription of an air
Duration: 3:50

Instrumentation: Standard instrumentation

Specific Requirements/Considerations: Little percussion; solo options

Instructional Concepts/Skills: Expression, line, breath control

General Comments: Students really enjoy this transcription of one of the most amazing melodies ever written.

—Submitted by Ted Hadley

Title: Cliff Island Suite
Level/Grade: 3
Composer/Arranger: Robert Jager
Publisher: Kjos
Classification: Three-part suite:
        1. Clambake
        2. Fog on Casco Bay
        3. "Aucocisco"—The Ferryboat
Duration: 6:50

Instrumentation: "Fog on Casco Bay" needs a large pipe to imitate a ship horn and/or a chime to imitate a ship's bell.

Specific Requirements/Considerations: No unusual problems

Instructional Concepts/Skills: Part 1 is happy music depicting a party. Tempo changes, including an accelerando, are called for. Part independence is important in each movement. Part 2 is a musical representation of a foggy scene, not technically hard but musically a challenge to represent. In Part 3, chromatic usage is evident. The piece presents the teacher with opportunity to stress "style."

General Comments: This is truly a clever little piece for young bands.

—Submitted by Ken Feneley

Title: Devil Dance
Level/Grade: 3
Composer/Arranger: John Kinyon
Publisher: Alfred
Classification: Tarantella
Duration: 3:00

Instrumentation: Standard instrumentation

Specific Requirements/Considerations: Several section solos

Instructional Concepts/Skills: This piece has 6/8 rhythms, including a pattern with a dotted eighth note, a sixteenth note, and an eighth note and a pattern with an eighth note and four sixteenth notes. Articulation and dynamics are important.

General Comments: This piece has an exciting rhythmic part contrasted with a slow middle section. There are interesting parts for all students.

—Submitted by Ted Hadley

Title: Dinosaurs
Level/Grade: 3
Composer/Arranger: Daniel Bukvich
Publisher: Phoebus
Classification: Contemporary/aleatoric
Duration: 7:00

Instrumentation: This piece calls for standard winds and a piano. Unusual percussion items are needed (stamping tubes, crystal stemware).

Specific Requirements/Considerations: Aleatoric sections, band singing, unusual instrumental techniques

Instructional Concepts/Skills: This piece can serve as an introduction to minimalism and aleatoric techniques. It calls for expressive playing; unusual instruments, techniques, and sonorities; and "visual" music.

General Comments: This piece makes effective use of late twentieth-century techniques. It is fun to play—enjoyable for band and audience. It demands musical discipline and self-discipline; it can also be used with high school bands.

—*Submitted by Ted Hadley*

Title: Fanfare, Ode, and Festival
Level/Grade: 3
Composer/Arranger: Bob Margolis
Publisher: Manhattan Beach
Classification: Dance suite
Duration: 4:00

Instrumentation: No special needs or problems

Specific Requirements/Considerations: No major problems

Instructional Concepts/Skills: This piece can be used to teach terraced dynamics, style changes, and Renaissance music. It calls for balance, blend, and precise intonation.

General Comments: Wonderful Renaissance dances

—Submitted by Marguerite Wilder

Title: Fortress
Level/Grade: 3
Composer/Arranger: Frank Tichelli
Publisher: Manhattan Beach
Classification: Concert piece
Duration: 5:00

Instrumentation: Standard with piccolo, E-flat clarinet, E-flat contrabass clarinet

Specific Requirements/Considerations: This piece has challenging percussion parts, an exposed trumpet solo, a flute solo, and a horn glissando. The ranges are moderate.

Instructional Concepts/Skills: This piece can be used to teach harmonic analysis (there is a student study sheet). Articulations are absolutely essential to correct performance. Dynamic contrast is also essential to performance. Intuitive sensitivity is required.

General Comments: Excellent program notes and aids for performance are included. This is another Tichelli masterpiece that adolescents enjoy; it will force them to be musical. It's totally creative: parts are important and scoring is open, not blocked. The students are literally "pulled" through to the exciting climax. This is a winner.

—*Submitted by David Reul*

Title: Irving Berlin's Songs for Americans
Level/Grade: 3
Composer/Arranger: Berlin/Swearingen
Publisher: Hal Leonard
Classification: Medley
Duration: 5:20

Instrumentation: The clarinet, trumpet, and trombone all have 3-way division. The clarinet range is to high C. The trumpet range is to high A with optional high C.

Specific Requirements/Considerations: Solos include snare, trumpet, flute, and clarinet. There are four time changes and three key changes. Transitions from song to song are not difficult but require rehearsal.

Instructional Concepts/Skills: Songs included are "This Is the Army, Mr. Jones," "Give Me Your Tired, Your Poor," "This Is a Great Country," and "God Bless America." This arrangement can be the basis for a lesson on Irving Berlin and all his music. It can also be used to teach transitions and key and time changes. There are many styles in this arrangement.

General Comments: Students are not exposed to this type of music enough; so that alone is a reason to program it. There is a lot of teaching material in one selection, and the students, as well as the audience, really enjoy the piece.

—Submitted by Dixie Detgen

Title: Kaleidoscope
Level/Grade: 3
Composer/Arranger: John O'Reilly
Publisher: Alfred
Classification: Contemporary compositional techniques
Duration: 2:30

Instrumentation: Overall range is typical for this classification.

Specific Requirements/Considerations: Interesting percussion parts include a xylophone. The piece also has nice French horn parts that are well worth working on. The range goes up to high G for flute.

Instructional Concepts/Skills: This piece can be used to introduce students to the concept of writing where the composer uses extensive accidentals rather than a key signature because of frequent tonality shifts.

General Comments: This is one of John O'Reilly's lesser known compositions. It is a very imaginative piece that students, once they learn about the compositional techniques, really enjoy.

—*Submitted by William Sutherland*

Title: March Forth
Level/Grade: 3
Composer/Arranger: Donald I. Moore
Publisher: Shapiro, Bernstein & Co.
Classification: March
Duration: 3:00

Instrumentation: Standard instrumentation

Specific Requirements/Considerations: The horn section is featured at the first trio statement. Good sections are needed across the band. At the second trio statement, there is a technical alto saxophone and clarinet obbligato part.

Instructional Concepts/Skills: The antiphonal introduction is rhythmically repeated prior to last trio statement. The piece uses the key of G-flat in the second strain. Wide dynamic levels are called for. Students must learn to mimic/copy articulation/tonguing styles from brass to woodwind and vice versa.

General Comments: This is a truly outstanding march for good junior high/middle school bands.

—Submitted by Ken Feneley

Title: March Juno
Level/Grade: 3
Composer/Arranger: John Stewart
Publisher: Shawnee Press
Classification: March
Duration: 3:30

Instrumentation: Standard instrumentation

Specific Requirements/Considerations: Good articulation skills and agility are needed by upper brass and woodwinds.

Instructional Concepts/Skills: Style, articulation, dynamics, expressive line

General Comments: This is a great British-sounding march with expressive melodies that are fun to play. It is a very effective concert march.

—*Submitted by Ted Hadley*

Title: Normandy Beach March
Level/Grade: 3
Composer/Arranger: John Edmondson
Publisher: Hal Leonard
Classification: March
Duration: 3:00

Instrumentation: No special needs or problems

Specific Requirements/Considerations: Flute: obbligato section

Instructional Concepts/Skills: There are many excellent sections for each instrument. The piece features a muted trumpet fanfare, a nice percussion interlude, a bass line and flute melody, and a good use of countermelodies for baritones and horns.

General Comments: The piece begins like a drum/fife selection. It is a very nice concert march for young bands.

—*Submitted by Marguerite Wilder*

Title: Pavane
Level/Grade: 3
Composer/Arranger: Fauré/McGinty
Publisher: Queenwood
Classification: Overture
Duration: 5:30

Instrumentation: Clarinet, trumpet, and trombone all have 3-way division. Range is up to high B for clarinet and up to high G for trumpet.

Specific Requirements/Considerations: This piece is full of soli passages, beginning with low flute and then passing to everyone. It has very exposed sections, but is extremely playable and teachable. The rhythmic figures are repetitious, and they get passed around from section to section.

Instructional Concepts/Skills: Independent playing is a must. The line is passed around within a phrase so students learn to be very phrase conscious. There are lots of accompaniment figures and ties across the bar lines.

General Comments: This piece is new, but is wonderful. The students love it and ask where they can get a recording of it. It has an enormous amount of teaching material to cover. This piece was commissioned in memory of a student in the band who was tragically killed in an auto accident. It fit the situation as no other piece of music could have.

—Submitted by Dixie Detgen

Title: Suite from Bohemia

Level/Grade: 3

Composer/Arranger: Vaclav Nelhybel

Publisher: Canyon Press

Classification (March,etc.): Four-part suite:

        1. Procession to the Castle

        2. Folktale

        3. Tournament

        4. Round Dance

Duration: 8:00

Instrumentation: This piece calls for standard instrumentation; the percussion section is very important.

Specific Requirements/Considerations: Exposed sections include the percussion section in Movement 4; the trombone section in Movement 3; and the woodwind section in Movement 2. Ranges are not extreme. Woodwinds must execute mordents in Movement 2.

Instructional Concepts/Skills: There are a variety of styles to understand. There is a true Bohemian flavor to each movement. A sudden tempo change occurs at the end of Movement 1. Modal scales and harmony abound in all movements, and percussionists must be adept in order to perform this piece.

General Comments: This piece calls for a variety of styles and soloistic and aggressive playing. This is truly outstanding music that is well constructed.

—Submitted by Ken Feneley

Title: Three Ayres from Gloucester
Level/Grade: 3
Composer/Arranger: Hugh Stuart
Publisher: Concert Works Unlimited
Classification: Three-part suite:
        1. The Jolly Earl of Cholmondeley
        2. Ayre for Eventide
        3. The Fiefs of Wembley
Duration: 4:30

Instrumentation: Standard instrumentation

Specific Requirements/Considerations: Clarinet solo and trumpet solo in Movement 1; horn section solo in Movement 2; flute section solo in Movement 3

Instructional Concepts/Skills: Great music for the young band—it has very demanding part and section independence. This is an exceptional arrangement of "British" music and worthy of the efforts of the very best young bands (and it can only be played well by accomplished groups). The 6/8 meter in "The Fiefs of Wembley" feels intrinsically correct so it can hardly be played wrong if the technique can be handled.

General Comments: Wonderful music—only the well-trained are able to do justice to this. It appeals to the heart, mind, and soul of the student-musician.

—Submitted by Ken Feneley

Title: Three Old American Ballads
Level/Grade: 3
Composer/Arranger: William E. Rhoads
Publisher: Wynn Music
Classification: Three-part suite:
        1. When the Work's All Done This Fall
        2. Poor Wayfaring Stranger
        3. Big Rock Candy Mountain
Duration: 7:40

Instrumentation: Standard instrumentation

Specific Requirements/Considerations: A flute solo begins and ends with "Poor Wayfaring Stranger." There is also a brief horn solo in the same movement. Each wind section is exposed at some point. Ranges are moderate.

Instructional Concepts/Skills: Various articulations/tonguing from staccato to legato are called for during this piece. Rhoads seems to be a master arranger of these kinds of selections for young bands. Melodies and countermelodies are interestingly adapted for players. Players must be well taught in order to be able to perform their independent parts.

General Comments: Its use of familiar melodies makes this piece interesting for students. The unique arranging abilities of Rhoads make the performance of this selection challenging, interesting, and musically satisfying.

—Submitted by Ken Feneley

Title: Variation Overture
Level/Grade: 3
Composer/Arranger: Clifton Williams
Publisher: Ludwig
Classification: Theme and variations
Duration: 6:00

Instrumentation: This piece calls for standard instrumentation and a range of Concert low B-flat to Concert high F.

Specific Requirements/Considerations: There are no individual solos. But there are several passages where trumpet I, clarinet I, and flute are scored for melody. Technical problems relate to chromaticism and accidentals within measures. Students find this piece challenging.

Instructional Concepts/Skills: This is a good piece for teaching students about theme and variations. It includes meters of 4/4, 3/4, and 2/4 and standard articulations: accents, staccato, slurs. It has various tempos: majestic, with quarter note = 92; then quarter note = 108; then quarter note = 96 (waltz); and at measure 101, quarter note = 132. Measure 129 to the end of this work requires a little extra effort as Williams brings his composition to a close. Rhythms are standard—the most difficult being a rhythm with an eighth note and two sixteenth notes.

General Comments: This piece provides students with the opportunity to discover the musical form of theme and variations. This piece works well when used in conjunction with a comprehensive musicianship project.

—*Submitted by T. Broyles-Brouillard*

Title: Cajun Folk Songs
Level/Grade: 3½
Composer/Arranger: Frank Tichelli
Publisher: Manhattan Beach
Classification: Folk songs
Duration: 4:30

Instrumentation: No special needs or problems

Specific Requirements/Considerations: The alto saxophone has a solo. The woodblock is extremely important.

Instructional Concepts/Skills: 5/4 to 3/4 mixed meter; excellent American heritage music; Cajun folk music

General Comments: The teacher should consider playing recordings of the music, which is available in vocal versions and in a version featuring Tichelli's arrangement on synthesizer. It is an excellent teaching piece for young bands.

—Submitted by Marguerite Wilder

Title: Cobb County Festival
Level/Grade: 3½
Composer/Arranger: John O'Reilly
Publisher: Alfred
Classification: Overture
Duration: 4:00

Instrumentation: No special needs or problems

Specific Requirements/Considerations: Oboe solo

Instructional Concepts/Skills: This is an excellent rhythmic piece. It offers exciting music and nice use of syncopation.

General Comments: This is a very nice overture with quality melodic material that students enjoy. It is good as a festival/contest selection.

—Submitted by Marguerite Wilder

Title: Dreams and Fancies
Level/Grade: 3½
Composer/Arranger: Timothy Broege
Publisher: Manhattan Beach
Classification: Four-movement suite
Duration: 5:30

Instrumentation: No special needs or problems

Specific Requirements/Considerations: No major problems

Instructional Concepts/Skills: This piece calls for 5/4 time in the fourth movement. It also calls for contrast of lines and hand-off style, forms, and melodies. There is very little tutti playing. Excellent textures, color, and mood changes are called for.

General Comments: This is wonderful twentieth-century music for younger bands. It has many different textures.

—Submitted by Marguerite Wilder

Title: Psalm Tune Variations
Level/Grade: 3½
Composer/Arranger: Jim Curnow
Publisher: Jensen
Classification: Theme and variations
Duration: 5:00

Instrumentation: No special needs or problems

Specific Requirements/Considerations: Temple block, solo trumpet

Instructional Concepts/Skills: This piece makes excellent use of theme and variations. Time signatures are 4/4, 3/4, and 6/8.

General Comments: Many styles and colors achieved in this piece, which is a good introduction to theme and variations form.

—Submitted by Marguerite Wilder

Indexes

Composer/Arranger

Title